智惠 女士 雅賞

子琬君

二〇〇九年
　月十七日

于琬君花鳥畫集

PAINTINGS BY
WINIFRED WAN-CHUN LEE (Nee YU)

序

藝術欣賞，當在立意、技法、與再現上著眼。

藝品有層次之分；臨摹只在修練技法，造型亦只在造一己之私，於人無涉；唯立意始有人間價值，不論文字、圖形、歌詠、舞蹈等媒體，始得不遭作賤。

向來立意，在「言之有物」。

孔子編春秋，在於警惕亂臣賊子；顧愷之之所以作女史箴，只為部分人類立下思想箴規、行為準則；李師訓藉青綠山水，以示河山並不承人主之志；王維深悟榮華無常，田園清趣存有上樂，始致力於「詩中有畫，畫中有詩」；馬蒂斯夢寐以求的是「一個有均衡、純淨、避免製造紛擾、或壓迫主體的藝術」（一九〇八）。畢卡索深覺「醜中無醜，是因醜中無惡」；「現實如能超脫，則較現實更現實」；「畫不存在於一度空間，是以多度空間更真實」。這些立意，自非清水無魚。而文如其人，終生踐履，莫過於畫竹始祖關羽，其臨竹建創虛懷與義薄雲天的堅貞，影響世界人口最多民族之深遠，豈祇「家喻戶曉」而已！

一次畫展中，為滿室「雅」、「歛」所懾。而筆涉工、皴兩造，且互動其間，尤使心儀；遂得識素手畫家于琬君女史。近細讀琬君十餘年累積畫作，更能深入解悟其立意真諦。琬君畫題雖以花鳥為主，然偶而弄皴，則山石豪闊。觀其立意，一貫在無求，雖千張萬幅，隱隱現現，伸手可擷。能無求則寡欲，寡欲則無貪。放眼世界，之所以一片紛擾，均因貪、縱所造成。少、青、壯年為之戕害，即在老耄，尤須「戒之在得」。立意無求，人性弱點，堵一大洞。蓋能無求，則貪、縱兩虎必悄然消失。果真如此，女媧之石，要它何用？

國畫傳統技法，大致分為兩徑，即所謂的工筆與皴法兩途。變則則千頭萬緒，自成章法。「曹衣出水」、「吳帶當風」乃早期工筆技法兩大濫觴；到徽宗已匯集到精刻細描了。過程中，自曹不興到吳道子，線條傳統不僅在風格上由寫實，轉為浪漫；並在形式上由顧愷之的「鐵線描」，到吳道子的「蘭葉描」，更發展到後來的「十八描」之多了。至於皴法，嚴格說應該是線條傳統由寫實轉入浪漫的副產品。其究竟是線條風格的轉換而帶起皴來，抑或是因組織人物畫的線條不足以表現人物背景裡「山水」而創造了皴，這都無關緊要。但皴在國畫裡所發生的衝擊，倒是不能不仔細省察的。討論皴法毋須討論它的種類，而須注意它在審美上的貢獻。因為由於有皴，中國畫才能邁進「靈」的世界。靈不是迷離神異，而是一種隱喻、悠遠、雅淨的感應，它永遠在作者與賞者之間，產生一種「言在意外」、「此時無聲勝有聲」，就如天人之間，無須語言，而天意暢通的「天何言哉？」的「無言之美」。靈就是此情此景、此人此事的橋樑。有了皴，就有了中國人審美的基礎—崇尚自然。在技法上，皴也作了「没骨」以後的發展，譬如潑墨、現代與後現代等的國畫技法裡，皴的確是它們的鋼架。可惜，從來畫家在技法上多走單邊。尤其「少從×大師遊，得×大師精髓」的畫人，因拘泥於×大師的些許畫藝，常常不是線，就是皴，造成國畫在技法上的僵局。琬君在不求表現上作了大表現。由於立意無求，加上奠基深厚的功力，那管得何家家法，是以能穿插於工筆與皴法之間，像作品的10號、14號、39號、44號等二十餘作品中，究竟是工筆了，還是皴了？抑是工、皴之外，另建琬君之法，識者自可一睹即明。

　　琬君立意無求，技法在傳統之外；而最可圈可點的，應該是她的再現。國畫再現法自謝赫起就已重視「氣韻」，以後講「神似」、「空靈」......不一而足。西方畫家，在再現上主張尤多，如古典、浪漫、現實、超現實、印象、後印象、立體、普普、表現等等、主義繁多，然一言以蔽之，就是再現方法不同而已。

　　琬君再現法，似得顧愷之真義，即「遷想妙得，以形寫神。」也就是著筆之前，將目的物從各種角度作仔細心靈凝觀、沉思，而求得確切心得，然後藉其形以「再現」其心靈。誠如張文通所説：「外師造化，中得心源」。但再現心靈也好，「中得心源」也好，必得遵隨程序，始可談再現，更始可談再現確切。傳統上的再現，一般以「栩栩如生」或「逼真」為滿足。但逼真並非比真，更不是亂真。而是抽取各類形體（包括無形）的靈犀或心竅，以「筆」、「墨」、「色彩」、「位置」、「傳移」等的「骨法」，以求得「氣韻生動」的再現。因此，靈犀才是表現的精髓。靈犀的表現，可分純靈、柔靈、空靈、巧靈。迄今為止，「名」畫家雖多，風格尤怪異，然僅在造型層次上巧奪巧靈之功。而如劉海粟、溥心畬等之擁有諸靈者，更屬少數。今日琬君之兼有純靈、柔靈與空靈者，確寔不可多見，確寔是難能可貴，值得推讚。

彭冊之

一九九七年九月於加拿大溫哥華

VIEWS OF ART

In the appreciation of art, three vital points of view should be stressed : those of theme, skill, and representation.

Artistic works can also be hierarchically classified into three levels:copying and imitation for the practice of skills, creation of forms or patterns for personal identification, and the development of artistic themes. The simple creation of forms and patterns may not be beneficial for the general audience, but themes can have universal value. The development of themes, in all senses, is aimed at "making sense." Media such as literature, drawing, painting, singing, or dancing should never be made cheap.

Confucius edited Chun-Oiu (Spring and Autumn)as a warning to those ministers or generals who rebel against their monarch, or collaborate with the enemy, and to those who do evil to people. The theme for Gu Kai-zhi's famous piece entitled "Ladies' Mores" is to set up a behavior code for half of the world's largest population. Li Shi-Xun used his popular "Qing-lu shan shui" (Indigo and Green Landscape) to demonstrate that land and water do not take orders from rulers. The insight that Wang Wei reached on the inevitability of the rise and fall of human lives, and the pleasure derived from country life made him create the so-called style of "There is painting in poems, and vice versa." Henri Matisse claimed that "What I dream of is an art of balance and purity, devoid of troubling or depressing subject matters" (1908). And Piccaso tried to say: Ugly is not ugly, for it has no evil in it; would reality be surpassed, reality can be more real; forms and shapes do not exist on one plane; things on multi-dimensions, therefore, are more real. These statements are truly insightful. But above all these is GuanYu, the first bamboo painter in Chinese art history. Guan was the most loyal general in Chinese history owing to his life's devotion to the theme of his painting which used the bamboo motif. Bamboo, he believed, was the true symbol of modesty, humility and solidity. His personality and perseverance have made him a figure of worship, with his codes of behavior becoming a model for all Chinese families.

My first meeting with Winifred Wan-chun Lee was at one of her solo exhibitions in Richmond, B.C. I was quite shocked by the instant flood of emotions from the exhibition hall. It took me a moment to realize it was the quality of refinement and inhibition, particularly in the use of colour, that aroused these feelings. This attraction prompted my desire to know more of Winifred Wan-chun Lee. A careful study of her work from the preceding fifteen years gave me an opportunity to better comprehend her real theme. Birds and flowers are her main objects, though her occasional landscape paintings are powerful. Looming throughout her works is the theme of a "free mind". Being free-minded is being free of the desire for possessions and begets no greed. In reality, the whole world today is troubled by greediness and permissiveness. This corrupts not only the young, but also the old. As a Confucius saying indicates : "elders should refrain in obtaining." The theme of the "free-mind" can neutralize both of them.

Traditional Chinese painting skills can be traced in two ways : linear and painterly, though there could be thousands of variations. The linear school can be traced to Cao Bu-xing (active in Wu State in the period of the Three-Kingdoms). Hui-zong, a Song Dynasty emperor (reign 1101-1125), made this a full-fledged school. In the middle of this period, a major change of course within the school was made by Wu Dao-zi (active during the Tang Dynasty). Wu romanticized the traditional realistic style form "steel-lines"to "orchid-leaf lines" and from there, the popular "Shi-Ba Miao"(Eighteen-drawing Ways) came into full use. The painterly method is a by-product of the transition from the traditional linear method to the romantic variation. It has been said that in order to paint the background for a figure portrait, traditional or romantic, lines were not relevant for contrast, particularly while landscape was used as the middle and/or background. The use of this painterly methodology is not as important as its artistic impact and its contributions to aesthetics, which should be carefully examined. Because of the painterly method, Chinese painting entered the realm of 'ling', a perception aroused by inspiration, spirit, efficacy, metaphor, and nimbleness. Ling always bridges the perception of the artists and that of their viewers, letting them communicate about the art they experience and creating a beauty of silence or nonlinguistic communication. The painterly method contributes much to Chinese painting in setting a solid aesthetic foundation -- nature-adoration. The development of the painterly method, especially after 'boneless' strokes, is truly the steel-structure of Po-mo(splashes of ink), modern and post-modern Chinese art. Unfortunately, Chinese painters have been too lazy to advance and jump out of their teachers' snares. They still walk in the path of the painting avenue and trap Chinese painting in a deadlock. Winifred, however, has made a great leap, although she did not wish to. Owing to her free-minded appeal, she strolls and winds about or above the two methods. Winifred's work in plates 10, 14, 39, 44, et cetera, twenty-five in all, has demonstrated an unnamed 'method' which can be called the Winifred Method.

Based on her "free-minded" theme, Winifred walked out of the Chinese skill tradition easily, though her most important contribution to bursh-painting is her special way of representation. Artistic ways of representation in the brush-painting tradition, "atmosphere and rhythm" was first emphasized by Xie He(active in South Chih Dynasty 551-577), hence, "spiritual similarity" and "nimble air," just to mention a few. In Western painting, artists have also had different methods of representation, whether Classicism, Romanticism, Realism, Impressionism, Cubism, Surrealism, Expressionism, Futurism, Abstract Expressionism, et cetera. In brief, however, they all are different means of artistic representation.

In her artistic creations, using her own way of artistic representation, Winifred caught the inspiration of Gu Kai-zhi's "Qian xiang miao de, yi xing xie shen," that is, before using the brush, study the object carefully and then think and imagine until you arrest an insight; represent the spirit by using forms or patterns. Accordingly, contemplation is the key to representing the spirit in the mind. Zhang Wen-tong(active in late Tang Dynasty)states: "Following the universe without, arrest the spirit of mind within." Representation with the relevant and adequate skill and contemplation, must still follow proper procedures of brushwork, inkwork, colouring, positioning, transforming, et cetera, in order to reach the representation with a lively atmosphere and rhythm deriving from nimble perception of subject matter. In short, the essence of artistic representation is based on nimble perception and a free comprehending mind, or simply LING. Such a LING may be concretely interpreted and classified as PURE LING, TENDER LING, ATMOSPHERIC LING and INGENIOUS LING. Many popular contemporary brush painters have manifested their ingenious ling only to the level of form and/or pattern creation. Very few of them like Liu Hai-su, Fu Xin-yu, et cetera, have achieved every artistic ling. It is rare to see a painter posessing pure, tender, and atmopheric lings like Winifred in the Chinese artists' community. And she deserves such exceptional commendation.

Jay Pat. Peng
September, 1997
Vancouver, B.C. Canada

目錄 Contents

圖 版
Plates

1. 紅蓮相倚渾如醉　絹本　1981
   Red Lotus　*on silk*　*30 × 30cm*

2. 花魁　絹本　1981
Unique　*on silk*　*30 × 30cm*

3. 玉容寒香冷　絹本　1981
Chrysanthemum (1)　on silk　30 × 30cm

4. 晚菊傲霜後　絹本　1981
Chrysanthemum *(2)* *on silk*　*30 × 30cm*

5.　春來花鳥情依依　絹本　1992
Chickadees and Dogwood　on silk　33 × 33cm

6. 並蒂蓮依　絹本 1988
Dragonfly and Calla Lily　on silk　32 × 32cm

7. 梨花春曉　絹本 1991

Finches and Pear Blossom　*on silk*　*34 × 34cm*

8. 花襲蝶　絹本　1995

Butterfly and Daylily　*on silk*　*34 × 34cm*

9. 馬蹄蓮　絹本　1994
Calla Lily　on silk　64×83cm

10. 循香　絹本 1994
Hummingbirds and Honeysuckle　*on silk*　*42 × 53cm*

Winifred Lee

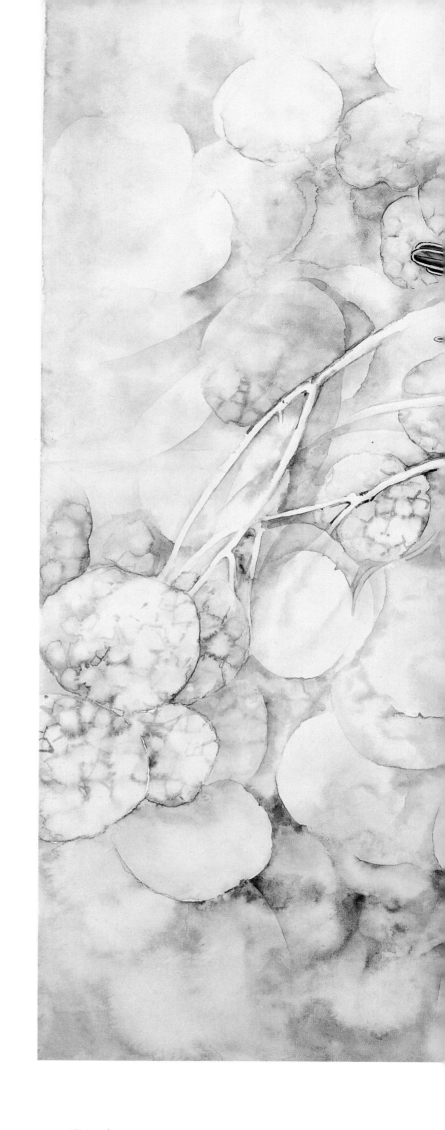

11. 緊相隨 1994
Red-Winged Blackbirds and Snow-ball Blossom *53 × 67cm*

Winifred Lee

12.　回首凝眸　絹本　1991
Oh, Hey!　*on silk*　*33 × 33cm*

13. 花間雙棲情無限　絹本　1992
Lovely Companions　*on silk*　*33×33cm*

14. 彩蝶舞芳菲　絹本　1993

Summer Dream　　*on silk*　　*49 × 86cm*

Winifred Lee

15. 蝶與波斯菊　絹本　1988
Butterfly and Cosmos on silk　30 × 30cm

16.　蝶來花有緻　絹本　1994

Butterfly and Sweet-Flowers　*on silk*　*33 × 33cm*

17. 鳶尾花　絹本 1983
Iris　on silk　30×30cm

18. 蝶與菊　絹本　1983
Butterfly and Mum　*on silk*　*30 × 30cm*

19. 粉紅百合　絹本　1988
Pink Lily　*on silk*　*32 × 32cm*

20.　賽牡丹　絹本 1988

Begonia　*on silk*　*32 × 32cm*

21. 紅豆相思訴衷曲　絹本　1988
Delightful Companionship　*on silk*　*32 × 32cm*

22.　罌粟花（一）　絹本　1988
Poppy（1）on silk　50×23cm

23. 罌粟花 (二) 絹本 1988
Poppy (2) on silk 33×33cm

24. 玫瑰 (一) 絹本 1989
   Rose (1) on silk 33 × 33cm

25. 玫瑰 (二) 絹本

Rose (2) *on silk* *33×33cm*

26. 吊鐘花　絹本　1989
Fuchsia　*on silk*　*33×33cm*

27. 嫣紅 1996
Fiery Red 68×11cm

28. 秋色 1996
Fall Colour 68×11cm

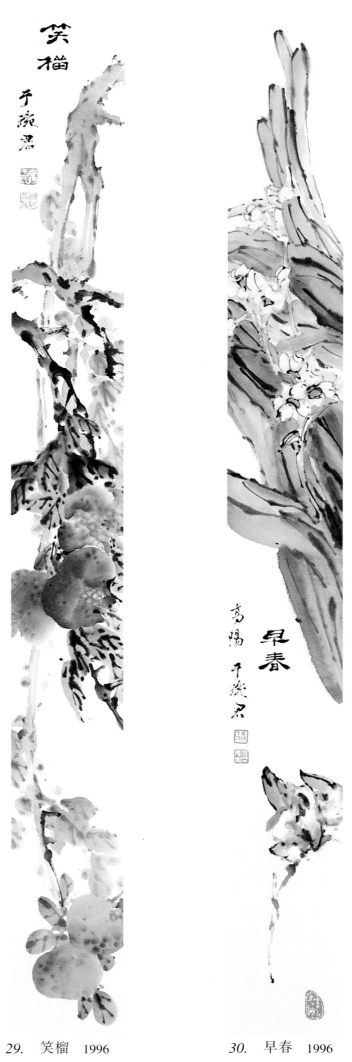

笑榴

于澂君

早春

高陽　于澂君

29. 笑榴　1996
Pomegranate
101×11cm

30. 早春　1996
Narcissus
101×11cm

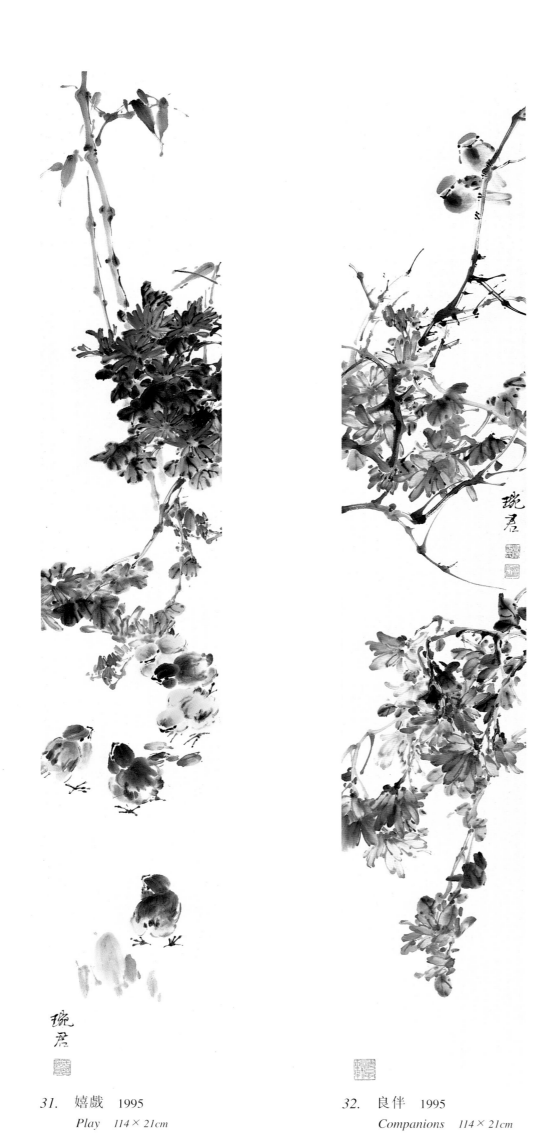

31. 嬉戲 1995
Play 114 × 21cm

32. 良伴 1995
Companions 114 × 21cm

33. 凝視 1995

Gazing At *114×21cm*

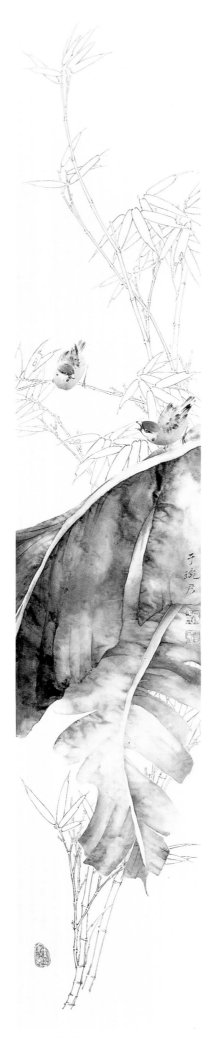

34. 蕉葉修竹　1995
Birds on Bamboo　*114 × 21cm*

35. 局部
    Partial

36. 涼風清水碧，荷氣雜天香　1995
Dragonfly and Lotus　*114 × 21cm*

58

37. 局部
Partial

38. 荷塘翠鳥　1995
Kingfisher with Lotus　*114 × 21cm*

39. 局部
Partial

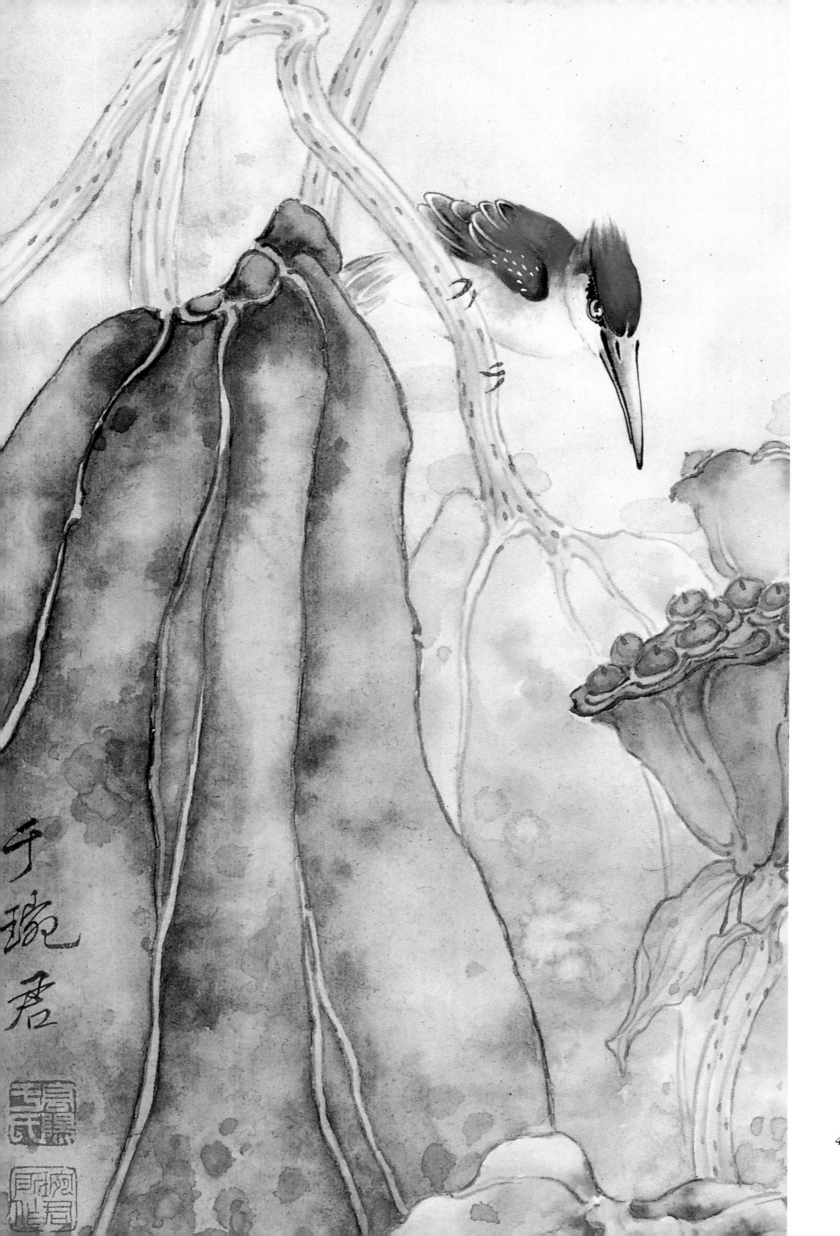

40. 局部 (41)
Partial

41. 荷花開盡秋光晚，留下枝椏果肥新
Bear Fruit　*114×21cm*　1995

42. 唯有牡丹真國色　1995
Tree Peony　*114×21cm*

43. 局部
Partial

44. 局部(45)
Partial

45. 國色天香 1995
Tree Peony with Butterflies *114 × 21cm*

46. 迎春　絹本 1996
Winter-Jasmine　on silk　53 × 20cm

47. 鳥語花香　絹本 1996
Lilac   on silk   53 × 20cm

48. 燕雙飛　1994

Two Swallows　*53 × 64cm*

49. 花間飛舞歌相喚　1995
Spring　*122 × 48cm*

51. 消夏 1995
Summer 122 × 48cm

53. 秋的旋律　1994

An Autumnal Melody　*122 × 48cm*

55. 鳳求凰　1994
Winter　122 × 48cm

56. 荷塘仙侶　1995
Mandarin Ducks in Lotus Pond　*122 × 48cm*

59. 梅下仙儔　1996

Lovely Couple Beside Mei Tree　*135 × 70cm*

60. 松鶴延年 (一) 1996
Longevity (1) 135×70cm

61. 松鶴延年 (二) 1996
Longevity (2) 135 × 70cm

62. 竹溪消夏　1996
A Summer Leisure Life　135 × 70cm

63. 野趣 (一) 1995
Wild Life *(1)* *65 × 95cm*

64. 野趣 (二) 1995
   Wild Life (2) 65×95cm

65. 翔 (一) 1992
Soaring *(1)* *50×66cm*

66. 翔 (二) 1992
   Soaring (2) 50×66cm

67. 雪中小憩 1991

Wood-ducks in Snow 51 × 68cm

68. 雙雁 1991

Canada Geese *51 × 68cm*

69. 母愛 1995

Motherly Love   *62 × 133cm*

71. 尋覓 1995

Beside the Bamboo *62 × 133cm*

72. 紫籐下　1995

Under the Wisteria　*134 × 68cm*

73. 群樂　1995
Happy Together　68×135cm

群樂

于琬尽 畫

74. 合家樂　1995

Happy Family　*133 × 62cm*

75. 迎風搖曳 (一) 1995
Dancing in the Wind (1) *120 × 70cm*

76.　迎風搖曳 (二)　1995
　　　Dancing in the Wind　(2)　120 × 70cm

77. 荷塘映月　1995

Moon's Reflection in Lotus Pond　*64 × 126cm*

78.　弄彩　1992
　　Lotus　66×43cm

79.　留得殘荷聽雨聲　1996

Lotus in Autumn　*69 × 69cm*

80. 人間仙境　1996
Mandarin Ducks in Lotus Pond　*67 × 131cm*

81. 婀娜多姿　1996
Graceful　69×69cm

82. 出淤泥而不染 1996

Lotus and Sparrows 69 × 69cm

83. 弄姿 1996
Charming 69 × 46cm

84. 冰清玉潔　1996
Chastity　*69 × 69cm*

85. 一塵不染　1985

Purity　*16 × 54cm*

116

86. 虞美人 1996
Poppy (1) *69 × 69cm*

87. 阿芙蓉 1989
    Poppy *(2)* *46 × 62cm*

88. 萱花　1993
Daylily　40×48cm

89.　卷丹　1988
Tiger Lily　46 × 55cm

90. 梅花報春曉　1988

Mei Blossom　*47 × 61cm*

91 借得雪梅一枝棲　1983

Snowy Mei Blossom　*52 × 52cm*

92. 老幹新枝　1995

Old Trunks With New Branches　*62 × 95cm*

93. 梅林曉月　1995

Morning Moon　62 × 95cm

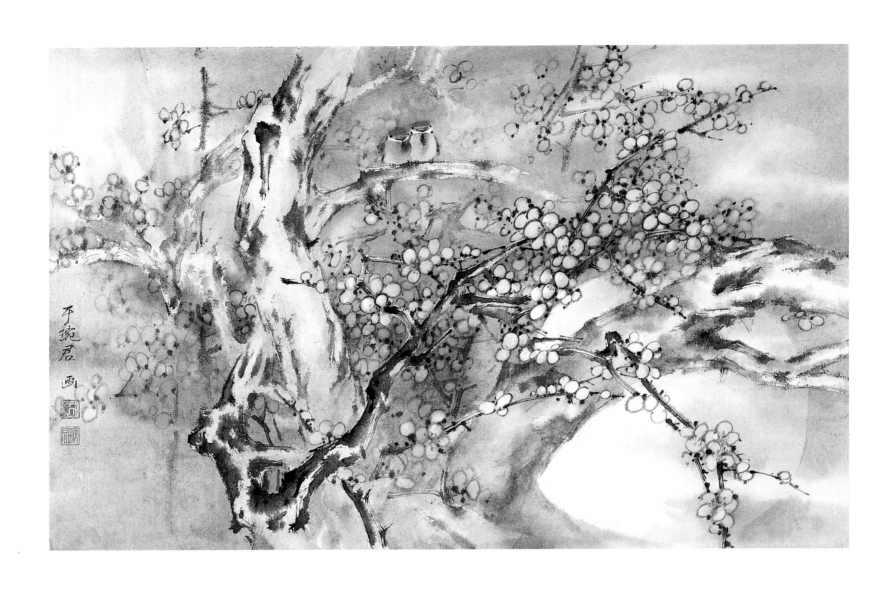

94. 滿月 1995
Full Moon 62 × 95cm

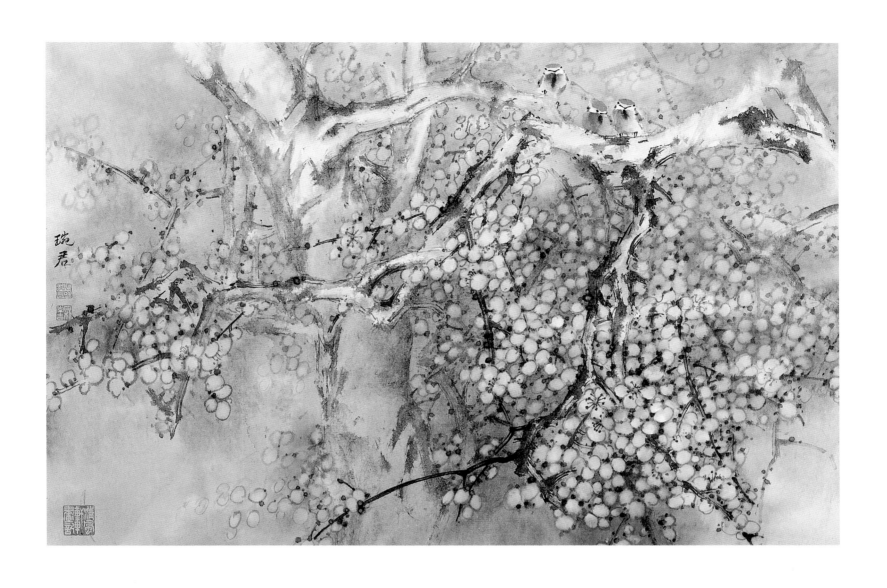

95. 春來花滿枝　1995
Early Spring　*62 × 95*

96. 不寒　絹本　1984
Warblers in Winter　on silk　27 × 27cm

97. 花引蝶　絹本 1985
Butterfly and Snapdragon　on silk　30×30cm

98. 相偎枝頭　絹本　1984
Finches on Dogwood　on silk　30 × 30cm

131

99. 六月花開時　絹本　1985
Dogwood Blossom in June　*on silk*　*40 × 50cm*

100. 稍歇　絹本 1985
A Break　*on silk*　*30 × 30cm*

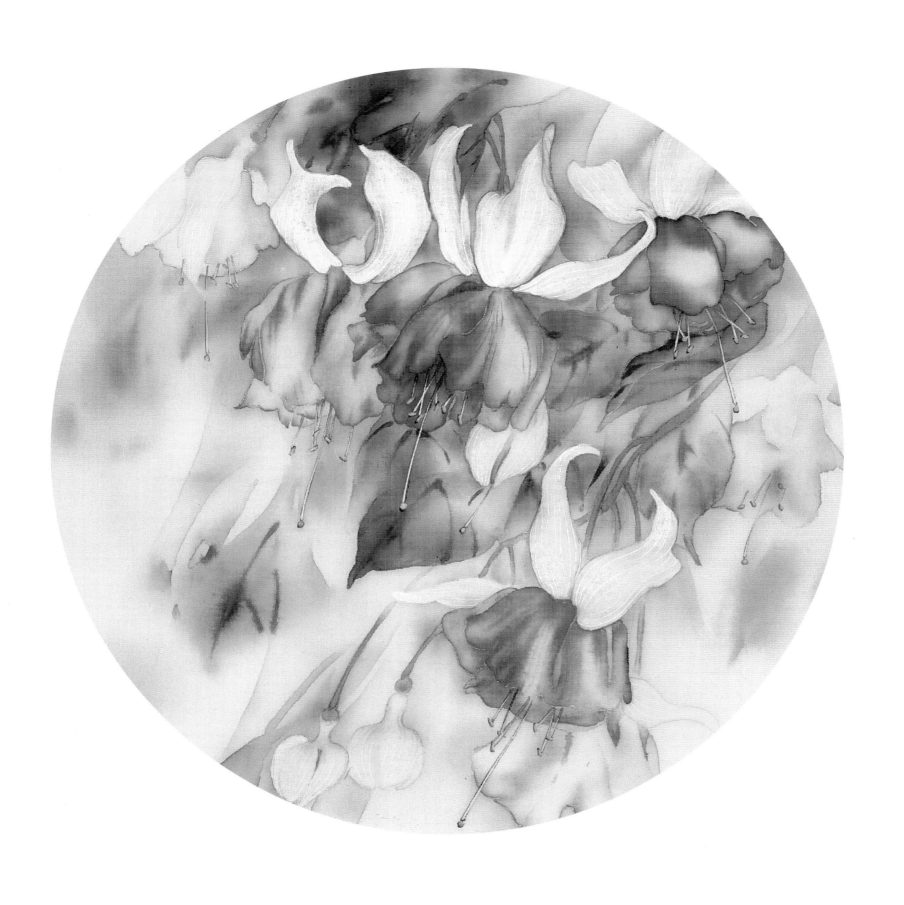

101. 吊鐘花　絹本　1989
Fuchsia　*on silk*　*33 × 33cm*

102. 冬雀　絹本 1984

Sparrows in Winter　*on silk*　*24 × 28cm*

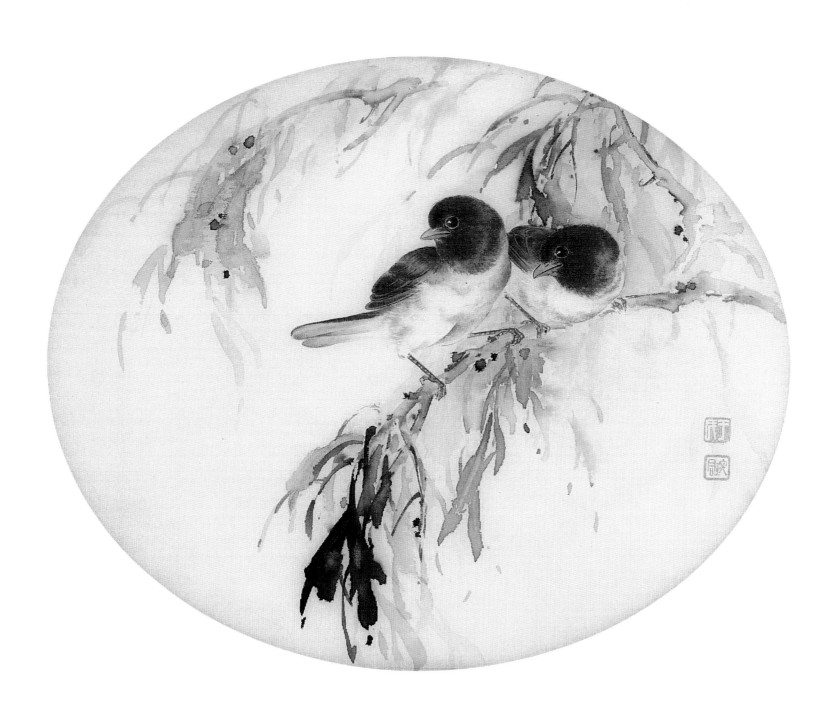

103. 春在柳梢頭　絹本　1984
Birds on Willow Twig　*on silk*　*24 × 28cm*

104. 賞雪 1993

Enjoy Snow Scenery *67 × 27cm*

105. 翠中翠 1993

Kingfisher and Lotus *67 × 27cm*

106. 修竹 1988
Bamboo *48×61cm*

140

107. 鳶尾花　1992
Iris and Butterfly　*61 × 30cm*

108. 雨竹　1988
Rain Bamboo　*48 × 61cm*

109. 秋塘即景　1992

A Glance at An Autumn Pond　*67 × 26cm*

110. 虎百合 1989
Tiger Lily *45 × 47cm*

111. 燈籠草　1989
Chinese Lantern　*56 × 25cm*

112. 紫鳶尾 1985
  Purple Iris 49 × 66cm

113.　辛夷（木蘭）　1986
Magnolia　*58×48cm*

114. 芍藥　1986
Peony　*58 × 48cm*

115. 紅鳶尾 1992
Red Iris *38 × 48cm*

116. 藍鳶尾 1992

Blue Iris 38 × 48cm

117. 天竺葵　1989
Geranium　*48 × 45cm*

118. 石楠 絹本 1988
Rhododendron *on silk* 44 × 55cm

119. 小聚　絹本 1987
Finches and Snow-Ball Blossom　on silk　44 × 55cm

120. 蝶與波斯菊　絹本　1989
Butterfly and Cosmos　on silk　34 × 34cm

121. 西洋蘭 1987
Orchid *on silk* *33 × 33cm*

122. 蜂鳥　絹本　1988

Hummingbird and Honeysuckle   on silk   34 × 34cm

123. 萱花 (一) 絹本 1989

Daylily (1) on silk 34 × 34cm

124. 萱花 (二) 絹本 1989

Daylily (2) *on silk* *55 × 18cm*

125. 萱花（三） 1992
    Daylily (3) 40×49cm

126. 玉立 1981

Slim and Graceful 84 × 66cm

Winifred Lee

127. 雄風 1981
Turkeys *84 × 66cm*

Winifred Lei

128. 菜之王　1985
Vegetables　24×39cm

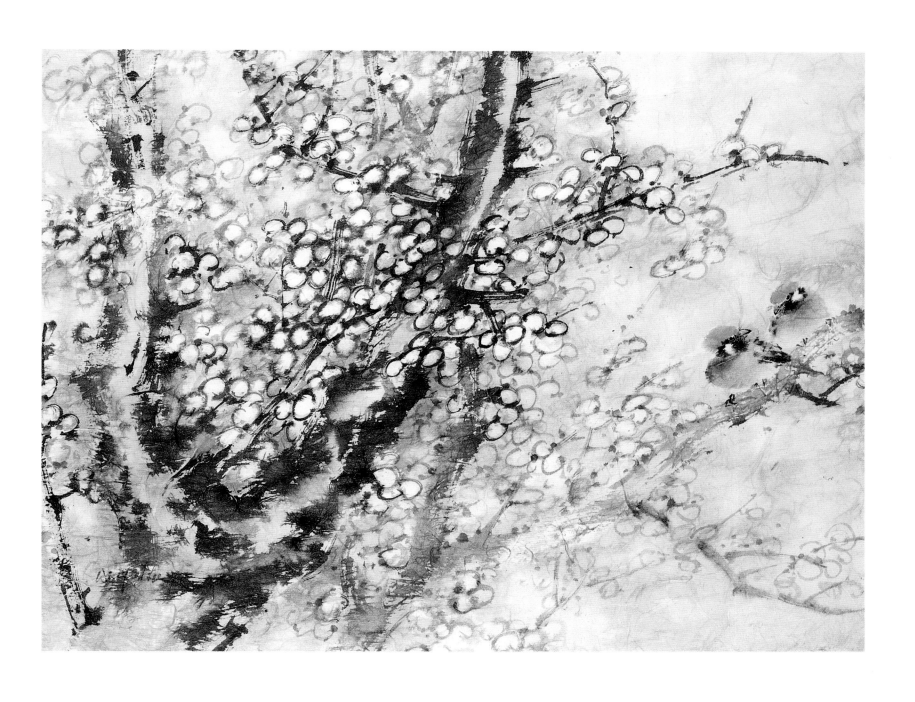

129. 梅花　1985

Sparrows and Mei Blossom　*40 × 50cm*

130. 藍繡球　1988
Blue Hydrangea　*51 × 68cm*

131. 鳥問花不語　絹本
Birds and Hydrangea　*on silk*　*45 × 55cm*

132. 黄鳶尾花　1995

Yellow Iris　*69 × 69cm*

133　緣藤　1995
Squirrel and Wisteria　122×48cm

174

134. 無言　1995

Birds and Wisteria　*68 × 35cm*

135. 排排坐 1995
Side by Side 69×69cm

136. 小憩　1995

Sparrows and Wisteria　*68 × 35cm*

137. 牡丹　絹本　1983

Tree Peony　*on silk*　*30 × 30cm*

138.　比翼雙飛　1996
Birds and Tree Peony　*60×89cm*

139. 春色滿園　1994
Brightness of Spring　*68 × 130cn*

140. 嬌 1996
Lovely *60 × 89cm*

141. 紅牡丹 1996
Red Tree Peony   *60 × 89cm*

142. 春到我家　1994
A Corner of My Yard　*68 × 130cm*

143. 花間繾綣　1996
Under The Shade　69 × 69cm

144. 白首雙棲　1996

An Affectionate Couple　*60×89cm*

146. 爭艷 1996
Competition *60 × 89cm*

李于琬君，祖籍河北、高陽。1934年生於北京。抗日戰爭時在四川、重慶度過童年，1948年隨父母遷居台灣，並在台灣接受中等及高等教育。1977年隨夫及三子移居加拿大溫哥華迄今。

WINIFRED WAN-CHUN LEE（Nee' YU）was born in 1934 in Beijing, China. She spent her childhood in Chongqing, the provisional capital of China during World War Ⅱ. In 1948 she moved to Taiwan with her parents where she completed her secondary and post-secondary education, and began her art studies in 1960 in private classes under several distinguished art professors. She immigrated to canada in 1977 with her husband and three sons, and settled in Vancouver down to the present. She is a member of the Richmond Chinese Painting and Calligraphy Club, a member of the Federation of Canadian Artists with an AFCA status, and a member of Vancouver Chinese Canadian Artists Association.

于琬君繪畫簡歷

1960-1964　期間在台灣從張義雄先生、喻仲林先生、吳詠香教授、孫多慈教授及黃君璧教授學習山水、花鳥、及素描。

1964　參加台灣第十九屆全省美術展覽，獲國畫組第一名。

1965　在台灣台北市中山堂舉行第一次個展。

1965　應邀參加　孫中山先生百年誕辰紀念　全國美術展覽
　　　　　　　　中 華 民 國 第 五 屆
　　　　　　（作品入藏歷史博物館）

1965　參加自由中國名家書法國畫展（在香港展出）。

1972　應邀參加第二屆全國書畫展。

　　　（中國畫學會，書法學會，及歷史博物館聯合主辦，在台北國家畫廊展出）

1973　應邀參加第二屆當代名家畫展。

　　　（中國畫學會及歷史博物館聯合主辦，在台北國家畫廊展出）

1973　應邀參加第九屆中日美術交換展。（中國畫學會及歷史博物館主辦）

1977　舉家移居加拿大溫哥華，次年在Douglas College進修西畫一年。

1979　與友人發起組織Richmond中國書畫學會。

1981　在溫哥華舉行移居加拿大後首次個展。

1981　在溫哥華自宅設立畫室，指導當地有同好之中西人士學習國畫，並常應邀到當地之其他藝術組織或學校，示範及講解中國繪畫。

1982　參加加拿大British Columbia省首屆美術節全省美展。

1982　在White Rock市舉行個展。

1983　參加溫哥華華裔藝術家傳統及現代美術展覽。

1984　加入加拿大藝術家聯盟為會員。

1985　參加加拿大藝術家聯盟1985冬季展覽獲獎。

1986　入選英國皇家水彩畫會與加拿大藝術家聯盟第一屆交換展。

　　　（先後在英國倫敦，美國西雅圖，加拿大溫哥華及維多利亞展出）

1987　在Surrey市舉行個展。

1987　參加加拿大藝術家聯盟第一屆巡迴展。

1987　在溫哥華舉行個展。

1988　在Richmond市舉行個展。

1989　參加Richmond書畫學會聯展。

　　　（在British Columbia大學亞洲中心展出）

1989　參加溫哥華華裔藝術家之蛻變展。

　　　（溫哥華中華文化中心主辦，加拿大政府贊助）

1990　參加美國Columbia Arts Centre與加拿大藝術家聯盟交換展。

1990　　參加加拿大藝術家聯盟90年水彩畫年展獲獎。

1990　　參加"The Conservation of Nature" Art Show.

　　　　（Sponsored by FCA and Nature of Trust of BC）

1991　　參加加拿大藝術家聯盟91年水彩畫年展獲獎。

1991　　獲加拿大藝術家聯盟授予AFCA頭銜。

1992　　參加加拿大藝術家聯盟92年冬季展覽。

1993　　參加加拿大藝術家聯盟畫廊新址開幕展。

1994　　參加發起溫哥華華裔藝術家協會，並參加該會首屆年展。

1995　　參加加拿大十二華裔畫家聯展，在台灣台北市國立藝術教育館展出。

1996　　參加加拿大十二華裔畫家畫荷聯展，在British Columbia大學亞洲中心展出。

1996　　在溫哥華青雲藝術中心舉行個展。

1997　　參加香港"慶三八，賀九七"中華百名女畫家聯展，在香港大會堂展出。

1997　　參加加拿大"十二華裔畫家"聯展，在溫哥華仲夏夜之夢畫廊展出。

1997　　參加旅加台灣藝術家作品聯展，在Burnaby之Shadbolt Centre for the Arts展出。

WINIFRED WAN-CHUN LEE'S
MAJOR PAINTING EXHIBITIONS

1964   "19th Taiwan Fine Arts Exhibition" at Taiwan Provincial Museum, Taipei
（Was awarded the first prize for Chinese painting）

1965   "5th National Arts Show in Celebration of the 100th Anniversary of Dr. Sun yat-Shen's Birthday" at National Historical Museum, Taipei
（Invited, jury-free; the work was collected by the National Historical Museum）

1965   "Exhibition of Well-Known Painters' and Calligraphers' Works of Free China" in Hong Kong.

1965   "Winifred Lee's Personal Painting Show" in Taipei.

1972   "2nd National Joint Exhibition of Painting and Calligraphy" at National Gallery, Taipei （Invited, jury-free）.

1973   "2nd Exhibition of Works by Well-Known Painters" at National Gallery, Taipei.
（Invited, jury-free）

1973   "9th Sino-Japanese Fine Arts Exchange Exhibition" in Tokyo, Japan （Invited, jury-free）

1981   "Winifred Lee's Personal Painting Show" at Richmond Art Centre, B.C. Canada.

1982   "Winifred Lee's Personal Painting Show" in White Rock, B.C. Canada.

1982   "British Columbia lst Art Festival Provincial Fine Arts Exhibition" in Kamloops, B.C. Canada.

1983   "The Exhibition of Traditional and Contemporary Visual Arts by Chinese Canadian Artists in Vancouver" at Robson Square, Vancouver, B.C. Canada.

1985   "Winter Show of the Federation of Canadian Artists" at FCA Gallery, Vancouver, B.C. Canada. （Received award）

1986   "First Exchange Exhibition of the British Royal Institute of Painters in Watercolours and the Federation of Canadian Artists" in Vancouver, Victoria （Canada）, Seattle （USA）, and London （England）.

1987   "Winifred Lee's Personal Painting Show" in Surrey, B.C., Canada.

1987   "Winifred Lee's Personal Painting Show" in Vancouver, B.C., Canada.

1987   "The 1st Traveling Show of The Federation of Canadian Artists"in various cities in Canada.

1988   "Winifred Lee's Personal Painting Show" in Richmond, B.C, Canada.

1989   "Exhibition of the Richmond Chinese Painting & Calligraphy Club"at Asia Centre, University of British Columbia, Canada.

1989   "Winifred Lee's Personal Painting Show" in Richmond, B.C. Canada.

1989   "In Transition: Chinese-Canadian Artists in Vancouver" Exhibition
（Organized by the Chinese Cultural Center of Vancouver, and funded by the Department of Secretary of State of Canada）

1990   "The Exchange Exhibition of the Federation of Canadian Artists and the Columbia Art Center of USA" in Canada and USA.

1990   "FCA 1990 Annual W atercolor Painting Show" at FCA Gallery, Vancouver, B.C. Canada.
        (Received award)

1990   The "Conservation of Nature" Art Show in Vancouver, B.C.
        (Sponsored by FCA and Nature Trust of BC, Canada.)

1991   "FCA 1991 Annual Watercolor Painting Show" at FCA Gallery, Vancouver, BC
        (Received award)

1992   "FCA 1992 Winter Show" in Vancouver, BC.

1993   "The Inaugural Show for the New Location Gallery of The Federation of Canadian Artists"
        in Vancouver, BC.

1994   "The First Annual Exhibition of the Vancouver Chinese Canadian Artist Association" at
        Vancouver Chinese Cultural Centre.

1995   "Joint Painting Exhibition of 12 Chinese Canadian Artists" at National Taiwan Art
        Education Center.

1996   "Joint Exhibition of LOTUS Paintings by 12 Chinese Canadian Artists" at the Asia Centre
        of University of British Columbia.

1996   "Personal Exhibition of Recent Paintings by Winifred Lee" at World-Wide Art Centre,
        Vancouver, BC.

1997   "Joint Painting Exhibition of the Hundred Chinese Lady Artists in Celebration of
        International Women's Day and Hong Kong's Returning to China" in Hong Kong.

1997   "1997 Annual Painting Show by 12 Chinese Canadian Artists" at The Midsummer Nights
        Dream Art Gallery, Vancouver, BC. Canada.

1997   "Joint Art Show of Taiwanese Canadian Artists" at the Shadbolt Centre for The Arts,
        Burnaby, BC. Canada.

國家圖書館出版品預行編目資料

于琬君花鳥畫集／于琬君著
Paintings by Winifred Wan-Chun Lee
：李鳳章，1997（民86）　面；公分

ISBN 957-97252-4-1（精裝）

1.繪畫—中國—作品集　　2.花鳥集—作品集

945.6　　　　　　　　　　86015112

于琬君花鳥畫集

發 行 人：李鳳章
　　　　　6471 MAPLE ROAD
　　　　　RICHMOND, B.C., CANADA V7E IG4
　　　　　TEL /FAX:(604)271-6606
攝　　　影：程大成
製版印刷：沈氏藝術印刷股份有限公司
出版日期：1997年12月
◎版權所有・翻印必究◎
國際標準書號　957-97252-4-1（精裝）

PAINTINGS BY WINIFRED WAN-CHUN LEE (Nee　YU)

PUBLISHED BY FENG-CHANG LEE
　　　　　6471 MAPLE ROAD
　　　　　RICHMOND, B.C., CANADA V7E 1G4
　　　　　TEL/FAX:(604)271-6606
PHOTOGRAPHED BY DAVID CHENG
PRINTED BY SHEN'S ART PRINTING CO., LTD.
PUBLISHED IN DECEMBER, 1997
◎ALL RIGHT RESERVED, NO PART OF THIS BOOK MAY BE REPRODUCED
ISBN　957-97252-4-1 (Deluxe binding)